Spooked

THE MOST HAUNTED PLACES IN THE WORLD

BY EMILY RAIJ

Reading Consultant:

Barbara J Fox
Professor Emerita
North Carolina State University, USA

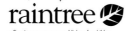

raintree

a Capstone company — publishers for children

Editorial Credits
Anna Butzer, editor; Kyle Grenz, designer; Morgan Walters, media researcher; Kathy McColley, production specialist

Printed in China
ISBN 978-1-474-70551-6
19 18 17 16 15
10 9 8 7 6 5 4 3 2 1

British Library Cataloguing in Publication Data
A full catalogue record for this book is available from the British Library.

Acknowledgements
Alamy: The Marsden Archive, 14, 15, toby de silva, 10, 11; Getty Images: PhotoQuest, 18, 19, Syfy, 27; iStockphoto: ImagineGolf, 12, 13, JohnGollop, backgroud 32; Shutterstock: D_D, (vintage photo frames) throughout, Balazs Kovacs Images, 28, 29, D_D, (paper notes) throughout, Dean Fikar, 6, 7, Delmas Lehman, 1, jan kranendonk, cover, kenkistler, cover, littleny, 22, 23, Marek Stefunko, 20, 21, Maria Dryfhout, 4, 5, Nickolay Stanev, 8, 9, Ross Strachan, 16, 17, Sociologas, (old photo strip) throughout, SSokolov, 2, 3, 30, 31, trekandshoot, 24, 25, Tueris, (grunge texture) throughout

CONTENTS

CREEPY CAUSES

Scraaaaatch! Is that a branch brushing up against the window or is your house haunted? Some people think ghosts are real. The following places around the world are famous for their haunted happenings.

THE ALAMO

In 1836, a bloody battle took place at the Alamo in San Antonio, Texas, USA. Hundreds of people died in the 13-day battle. Today, visitors claim to see the **spirits** of dead soldiers walking around this famous place.

spirit soul or invisible part of a person that is believed to control thoughts and feelings

DID YOU KNOW?

The Alamo was originally built in the 1700s as a place of worship.

ALCATRAZ ISLAND

In 1934, officials opened a prison on Alcatraz Island in San Francisco, USA, for the toughest **criminals**. Many prisoners died there before the prison closed down in 1963. Guards and prisoners reported strange sounds, smells and sights. Many believe that Alcatraz is still haunted.

DID YOU KNOW?

The **gangster** Al Capone is the most famous ghost believed to haunt Alcatraz. He sometimes played the banjo. Some visitors claim to have heard banjo music in the shower room.

criminal someone who commits a crime

gangster member of a criminal gang

AMITYVILLE HOUSE

In 1974, Ronald DeFeo Jr killed his family in their home in Amityville, New York, USA. George and Kathy Lutz bought the house in 1975. They heard strange noises and felt sudden temperature changes. After 28 days the Lutz family left the house in fear of ghosts. Was this a **hoax** or a real haunting?

hoax trick to make people believe something
that is not true

BANFF SPRINGS HOTEL

Banff Springs Hotel in Alberta, Canada, opened in 1888. Several ghosts are said to haunt this hotel. One ghost is said to be a bride who died falling down a staircase. Other guests report seeing ghosts of a murdered family and a dead **bellman** called Sam.

bellman someone employed to run errands and carry luggage around hotels

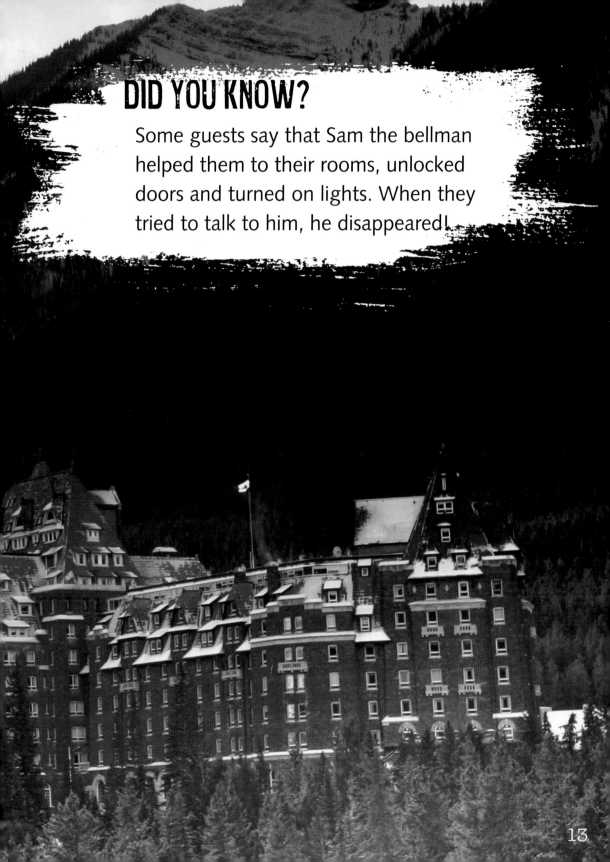

DID YOU KNOW?

Some guests say that Sam the bellman helped them to their rooms, unlocked doors and turned on lights. When they tried to talk to him, he disappeared!

BORLEY RECTORY

The Borley **Rectory** in Essex was said to have been haunted from the time it was built in 1862. Residents and visitors to the house reported ghosts, eerie footsteps and found mysterious bones. Stones were thrown when no one was around. The rectory burned down in 1939.

DID YOU KNOW?

Researchers studied the strange activities at the Borely Rectory. Some of the activities cannot be explained.

rectory house where the rector of a church lives

researcher someone who studies a subject to discover
  new information

15

EDINBURGH CASTLE

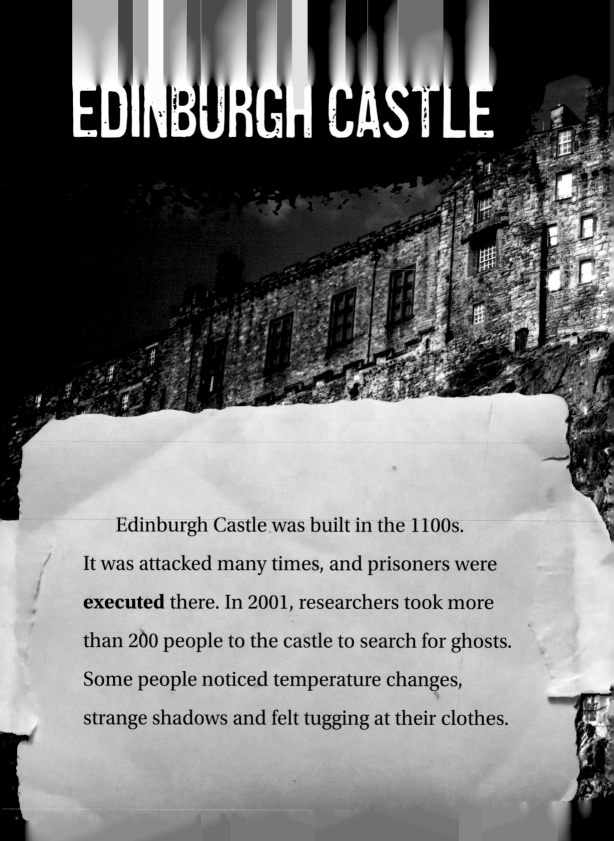

Edinburgh Castle was built in the 1100s. It was attacked many times, and prisoners were **executed** there. In 2001, researchers took more than 200 people to the castle to search for ghosts. Some people noticed temperature changes, strange shadows and felt tugging at their clothes.

execute put to death as punishment for a crime

GETTYSBURG

One of the bloodiest battles of the American Civil War took place at Gettysburg, Pennsylvania, in 1863. Thousands of soldiers were killed in just three days. Today, visitors report seeing ghosts of soldiers on the site of the battlefield as well as guarding Gettysburg College.

THE TOWER OF LONDON

The Tower of London was built in the 1000s. It was used as a prison and place of execution. Anne Boleyn, the second wife of King Henry VIII, was executed there in 1536. Some people believe they have seen and felt her spirit rush past them.

DID YOU KNOW?

The Tower of London is not actually a tower. It is an entire castle.

THE QUEEN MARY

The *Queen Mary* is currently a floating hotel in California, USA. It was used as a warship during World War II, and visitors report seeing sailors' ghosts. There are also reports of hearing the voices of two girls who drowned in the hotel pool. Guests also say spooky things happen in the kitchen where a cook was killed.

At the beginning of World War II, the *Queen Mary* was painted grey and given the nickname the "Grey Ghost".

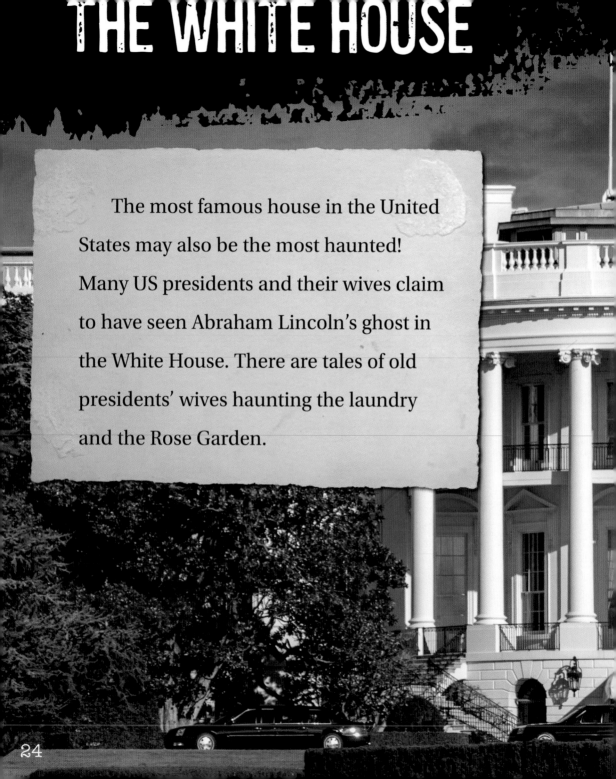

THE WHITE HOUSE

The most famous house in the United States may also be the most haunted! Many US presidents and their wives claim to have seen Abraham Lincoln's ghost in the White House. There are tales of old presidents' wives haunting the laundry and the Rose Garden.

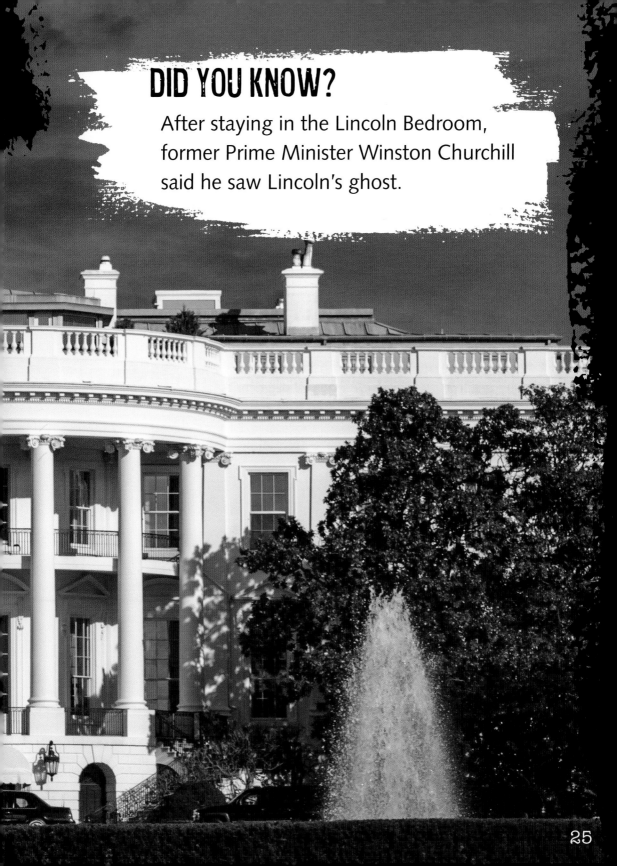

DID YOU KNOW?

After staying in the Lincoln Bedroom, former Prime Minister Winston Churchill said he saw Lincoln's ghost.

PARANORMAL INVESTIGATORS

Paranormal investigators study haunted houses. They take photos and record strange sounds or temperature changes. Sceptics say there is no proof of hauntings. Natural causes can explain strange sights, sounds and feelings.

paranormal investigator someone who studies events that science cannot explain

sceptic person who questions things that other people believe to be true

proof facts or evidence that something is true

DID YOU KNOW?

Investigators say the temperature can drop 5.6 degrees Celsius (10 degrees Fahrenheit) when a ghost is in the room.

HAUNTED OR NOT?

There is no way to know for sure if ghosts exist. Some **mysteries** turn out to be hoaxes while others are harder to explain with science. Either way, it's fun to wonder if spooky spirits are real! Perhaps one day you'll get to visit a haunted place. Perhaps you already have!

mystery something that is hard to explain or understand

GLOSSARY

bellman someone employed to run errands and carry luggage around hotels

criminal someone who commits a crime

execute put to death as punishment for a crime

gangster member of a criminal gang

hoax trick to make people believe something that is not true

mystery something that is hard to explain or understand

paranormal investigator someone who studies events that science cannot explain

proof facts or evidence that something is true

rectory house where the rector of a church lives

researcher someone who studies a subject to discover new information

sceptic person who questions things that other people believe to be true

spirit soul or invisible part of a person that is believed to control thoughts and feelings

BOOKS

All About Henry VIII (Fusion History), Anna Claybourne (Raintree, 2014)

Ghosts (Usborne True Strories), Paul Dowswell and Tony Allan (Usborne Publishing, 2008)

Ghosts and Hauntings (Solving Mysteries with Science), Jane Bingham (Raintree, 2013)

WEBSITES

www.bbc.co.uk/history/historic_figures/lincoln_abraham.shtml
Find out more about US President, Abraham Lincoln.

www.bbc.co.uk/history/people/anne_boleyn/
Discover more about Anne Boleyn's life and death.

www.hrp.org.uk/TowerOfLondon/
Explore the Tower of London and see if you believe the ghost stories!

INDEX